Hello,
my name is Mike.

I would like to show
you
that making mistakes
isn't bad!

Yesterday, I was at school, and you know what?
I did my homework completely wrong!

But my teacher told me that we learn from mistakes!
Yes, that's true!

At first, I didn't understand that.
After all, how can we learn from mistakes?

Now I know that when I do something wrong, I have to correct it. Thanks to this, I learn!

When you make a mistake
and don't know how to
solve it, ask your parents
or friends for help!

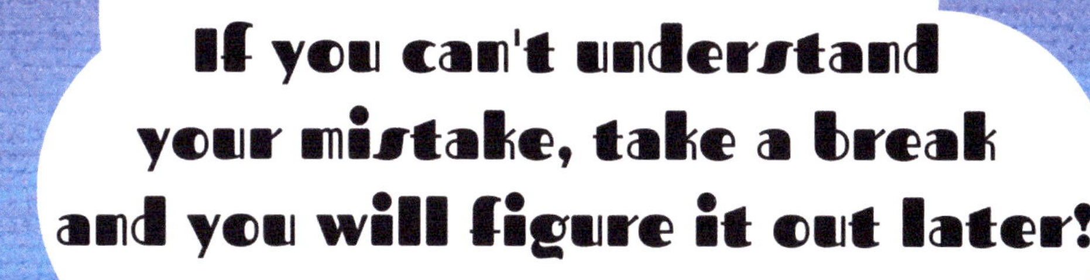
If you can't understand
your mistake, take a break
and you will figure it out later!

You can go for a
walk with your dog!
WOOW
WOOW!

When I don't understand a mistake, I stretch!
It always makes me will better!

When I make a mistake,
I try to learn
about it!

When I play the piano, I try not to make any mistakes.
However, when I make one, I immediately stop and correct myself.

When I was
at the playground
I wanted to show off
in front of
my friends.

I jumped off
the spinning carousel,
but it was very dangerous
and I will never do that
again.

Once I went to the forest by myself and got lost. Now I know not to do that anymore.
Fortunately, a little raccoon helped me find the way!

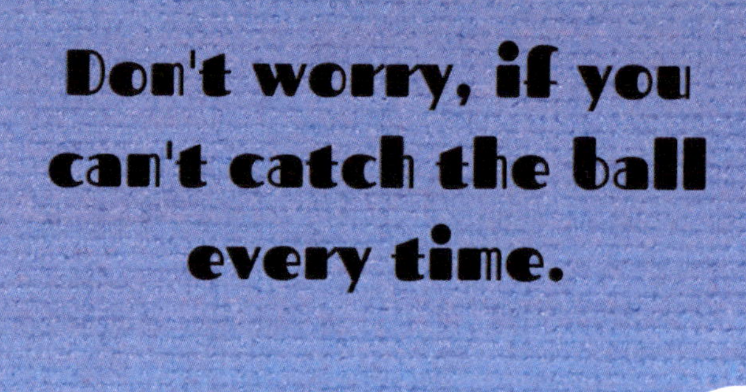

I can't catch it!

You will learn!

If you fall down, that's okay! Every time, you will get better.
However, be sure to wear athletic support.

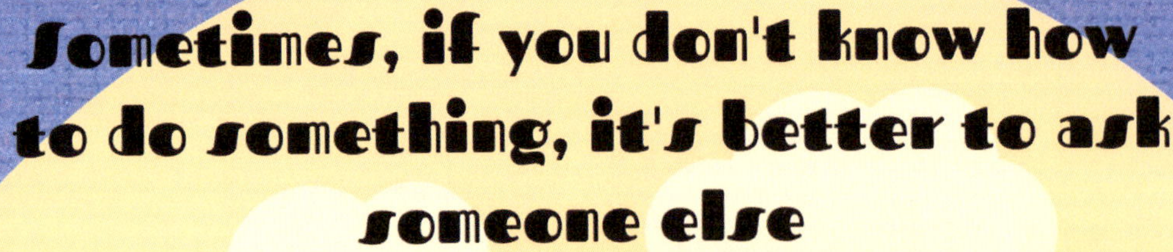
Sometimes, if you don't know how
to do something, it's better to ask
someone else

Kids, there is a
road nearby, let me
help you get through.

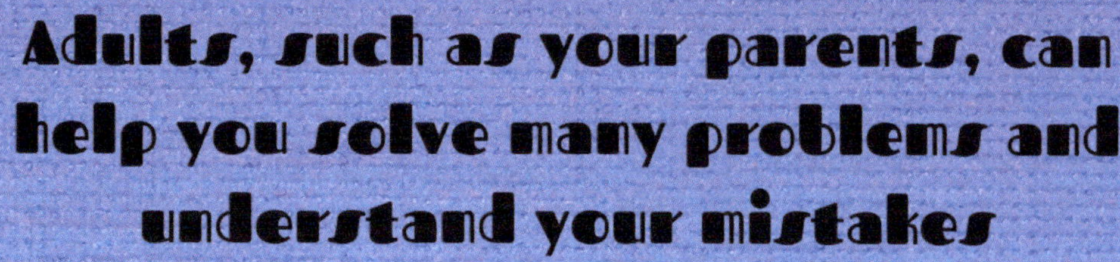

Baby, if you have any questions please tell me. I am always there for you!

You are doing great, but you can add even more pepper if you want it to be tastier!

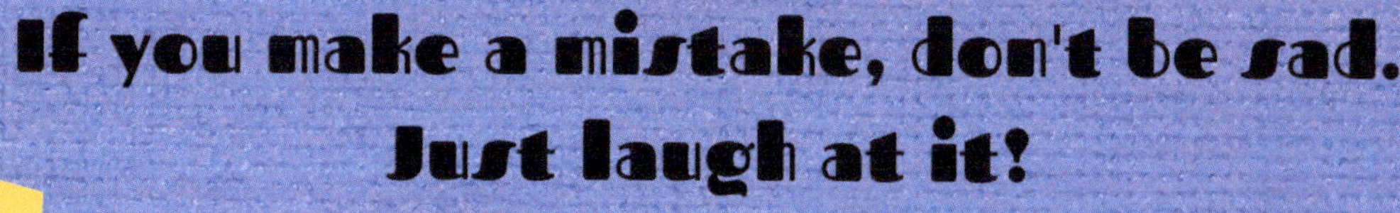

Ohh! I missed it!

That's okay, I often miss too!

Ohh! I slipped. I have to watch my steps next time!

Honey, you put too much water in the flower.
Remember not to overdo it.

I've been practicing this figure for a long time, but I don't give up! I can handle it!

This time
I can go down!

Oh no!
I sang the song
wrong. I'll start
from the beginning!

Remember, everyone
makes mistakes!
There is nothing
wrong with it!

Printed in Great Britain
by Amazon